Care Enough to Know
Keep Your Parents Safe

If you are even thinking of, planning on, or may ever consider a senior living community (independent living, assisted living, nursing care, memory care) for a loved one, **you need to read this book!**

In Memory of

Deron Andrew Mills
December 1, 1962 - September 23, 2008

Caring, giving, friend to countless individuals who he
happened to meet on a daily basis, Deron looked for a
need and then found a way to fill it. He blessed many
by doing charitable acts of providing food, clothes,
plumbing, Bibles, a place to stay and at least once, a
bicycle for transportation. He reached out to those who
could not, or did not know how (particularly the elderly).
He had a servant's heart, he was my son. I learned
volumes from him.

Contents

Acknowledgements

Thanks to my husband, Jim, for his patience, encouragement and unending support.

Also, thanks to all of my family members who were supportive of my efforts and confident that I could put this work together.

Special thanks to my son, David Mills, for his diligent nudging and faith in me to get this book written.

Thanks to my many associates over the years who by example have taught me about the senior living business.

Thanks also to my granddaughters, Jennifer and Amy for doing the book layout and artwork, and Clara Clark of clarityphotography.

Forward

If you are even thinking of, planning on, or may ever consider a senior living community (independent living, assisted living, nursing care, memory care) for a loved one - you need to read this book!

You might be the adult child or other family member assigned to the task of finding senior living for your parents or other loved ones. This role will not only require sensitivity, understanding and respect, but a great deal of patience as you coach your loved one through this major life transition. Not enough can be said for the many emotions that surface at a time such as this when one is facing "giving up" all that has been familiar and a normal part of every day life.

There are many things that the general public does not know about the Senior Living Business.

The information in this book will help you to uncover the truth and help you to make an informed decision resulting in a positive outcome.

Early in my twenty-five year career in the retirement business I began to feel a gnawing, underlying sense of dissatisfaction. This resulted from my observation of the gap between services promised and services delivered to residents moving into senior living communities. In many cases I have seen the "bottom line" mentality take precedence over what was really best for the residents.

When considering any type of a senior living care community, without a doubt, most people understand that "it will never be like home." However, it can come close if appropriate research is done beforehand.

My role as Marketing/Community Relations Director in various communities across the nation has been to find a need and fill it. This has included encouraging members of a somewhat vulnerable age group (56 and up) to make a major life change by moving into some type of congregate living for seniors. I moved these people in with a clear conscience, thinking that I was helping them and believing that they would receive the services as promised.

Over the years there was just enough promise to keep me believing that I had the residents' best interest at heart. In many cases this turned out to be true, but in other instances I found myself cringing in the face of reality as I observed the poor quality of service provided to folks I had promised a better life to... folks who trusted me.

This has bothered me to the point of knowing I must speak out. I feel it would be remiss of me to stand by and do nothing. That is my sole purpose for writing this book.

People need to know what to ask, what to look for and what to do when researching senior living communities.

I am offering guidance, direction and concrete ideas on how to achieve these three major tasks.

Very often family members or friends are thrust into the position of making a decision regarding senior care. This confusing maze of retirement/senior living community options can be discouraging. Before making a selection you are expected to know all possible options available. Without prior knowledge this can be an overwhelming, and what seems like, an insurmountable task. With some pre-cautionary steps and planned research the sense of mystery can be extracted from this process and a good decision can be made.

As I share first-hand knowledge gained over a 25-year period I will provide a step-by-step process to simplify your search. Experience with clients, adult children, doctors, various service-providing organizations, and other senior related entities has given me a complete picture of what is realistic and fair to expect. I am sharing what I have learned to aid you in making a sound, educated decision.

Of course there are no guarantees in any situation, but in this business it is definitely "what you don't know that can harm you."

While some of my suggestions may seem a little too invasive or nit-picky, they are important and necessary. We have all heard the horror stories about retirement communities and sadly enough many of them are true. Don't let your story become one of them!

I will address the common feelings, thoughts and a wide range of perplexities that families may experience as they begin the senior living community search. While searching you will come upon some issues that can be considered possible "red flags." See the list in the back of the book.

Real life stories have been included as well to bring reality to the reader's search for the best situation. An assessment tool on levels of care has been included in Chapter 7 to help in determining the appropriate level of care and community type.

My hope is that your journey through this process will be educational and enjoyable, resulting in a happy life-enhancing environment for your loved one.

It has been said: "Any man who knows all the answers most likely misunderstood the questions."

So, congratulations on your decision to learn more about how you can make the best retirement choice for yourself or a loved one!

Information reported in this book about incidents and occurrences in various communities did happen, was witnessed by me, and is conveyed to the reader not to alarm, but to suggest caution in certain areas.

All names, with the exception of authors of various books and quotations, are fictitious.

Chapter One
Know How to Begin

In all matters, before beginning, a diligent preparation should be made.

-Marcus Tullius Cicero

This chapter will cover the actual process that needs to be followed in order to make a complete and accurate check of any Senior Living Community that is being considered. Outlined below are the suggested steps. Each area discussed will be expanded upon in subsequent chapters. If you have received recent information that an immediate move is necessary you will not have time to do some of the steps listed below. If you are looking for future placement and have the opportunity to take a leisurely pace, more time can be spent following each step carefully.

Helpful Hints on How to Begin the Process

1. Keep in Touch with your loved ones. Know how they are doing. Look for any signs that they might need help.
2. Begin looking for a community before need dictates it.

3. Act at the right time. If sickness occurs it might provide an opportunity to consider options.

4. Be honest about the need and talk to your loved one about it.

5. If there is an immediate need for assisted living or skilled nursing ask the physician for some references in the area.

6. Visit communities to see what is available. Then, take your loved one to visit a few communities with you. If you find one that might work, get on the wait list.

7. Put a refundable deposit down to guarantee a spot for the future.

8. Once on the Wait List, visit often and work toward a move-in date.

9. Visit friends who have moved into a community.

10. Talk about the positive aspects of community living, i.e., friends to do things with, security, ready access to medical facilities and transportation.

11. Do everything suggested in Chapter 4 of this book. *Ask, Look and Do!*

12. Once the move-in date is established sell the house or give notice at current location.

13. Begin to downsize if necessary.

14. Procure a recent Physicians Report and list of medications. These will be required prior to move-in.

15. Make the move!

Chapter Two
Who Should Live in a Senior Living Community (SLC)?

A prudent question is one-half of wisdom.

-Francis Bacon

You might be wondering just who needs a Senior Living Community (SLC) anyway! Since God has made us all unique, each of our questions will be answered differently, and will fit each of our specific needs.

Maybe you have gotten that alarming call in the middle of the night that mom has been admitted to the hospital. Or possibly you have been watching your parents age and realize that they are in need of some daily assistance. It could be that your loved one will be best served by staying at home with a caregiver. However if this option is selected, there are some key considerations - safety, nutrition and socialization would be at the top of the list.

The physician should be involved in this decision. If it is decided that staying at home is not possible, consideration of a good Senior Living Community may be the answer. In that case, read on.

In the best of circumstances the subject of moving to independent living, assisted living, and extended care services would be brought up and discussed long before the need arose. It is not a bad idea to educate oneself while your loved ones are still very independent and healthy. One good way to do this is to take a leisurely afternoon drive and stop by a few places for a visit. Usually an appointment is not necessary. All you need do is walk in and ask to see the marketing or admissions person.

Most retirement communities are limited to age 55 and older. People move in for various reasons. The younger residents that I have met are usually those who have found themselves alone due to death of a spouse or divorce, or because they have chosen to remain single and want community-based living. And many of them still hold down full-time or part-time jobs. Some couples choose retirement communities because one spouse has some health issues. Others just don't want the responsibility associated with home ownership. Whether it's a large building with individual apartments or cottages, knowing there is always someone else around provides a sense of safety and security for any resident.

It is very common for women to be more willing to make the move than men. Perhaps it is because they typically do most of the cooking, cleaning and shopping and they are ready for a break! While we all prefer to make our own choices, in some instances the move may be a need-based decision. At that point it becomes a "decision of the will and not of the heart."

Issues listed below may be indicators of a need or a desire to look into a senior living community.

Poor or declining health
Inability to bathe, groom, eat, walk, take medication
Prolonged depression or loneliness
Frequent falls
Frequent forgetfulness
Weight loss
Chronic pain
Substance abuse
Inability to coordinate medications
Inability to pay for home care
Unsafe home atmosphere
Loss of appetite
Loss of interest in cleanliness
Inability to ambulate
Housebound
Just don't feel like cooking, cleaning, paying bills

A move to Assisted Living or Nursing Care is based on need. But a move into an independent community is a good option for those who don't necessarily need a lot of help but want more freedom, the ability to leave their home unattended for periods of time, or a relief from the cares of home ownership. Moving to a Skilled Nursing Facility (SNF) is determined by a physician and the resident has no choice.

Attention Caregivers!

If you are caring for a parent or elderly loved one, you are a key person in knowing their needs. Caregivers frequently experience burn-out and subsequently, failing health from the constant draw on their emotional, mental and physical health. Not only do your loved ones or friends have needs, but you do too. If you have been, or are currently the caregiver, your needs may dictate a change in living arrangements for your loved ones.

Although the thought of placing them in an assisted-living community is not something many people like to consider, it is important to be prepared for this option. It can lessen the stress level for the entire family by making such a move. This should not be construed as a negative step to take, rather a preventative measure for both you and those you are caring for. (Jacobs, Barry 2006).

You may have a family and a career in addition to your caregiving duties. It is important to encourage your loved ones to be as independent as possible both for their sake and yours. Most adult children or caregivers have no healthcare training and can be bogged down by the demands of loved ones who are unable to take care of themselves. (Hutchinson, Joyce, Rupp, Joyce 1999).

Various types of communities are available. The next chapter describes some of the various options. There is also a sample screening tool in Chapter 7 - *Know How Care Levels are Determined* - to help determine level of care needed by your loved one.

Chapter Three
Know the Choices

If you want a wise answer, ask a reasonable question.

-Johann Wolfgang Von Goethe

This chapter covers the different types of retirement communities and will help you to make the best choice for your loved one. If you are the adult child this will probably be one of the most difficult things you will ever do.

Fear of approaching your parents, guilt, depression, sorrow, lack of information and feeling overwhelmed are common to people placed in this situation. Not only will this be an emotional decision for you, but for the entire family and other loved ones. There is support available from various agencies. And, of course, churches, friends and others who have experienced the same issues should be willing to help.

One good resource for senior living communities is to contact the senior services agency or the Area Agency on Aging in the preferred area (list in back of book). Their staff will be able to give you information on the senior resource material and publications that are available.

There are also many online resources under the headings of Senior Living, Retirement Communities, Assisted Living and Continuing Care Retirement. The local yellow page advertising is helpful as well.

Independent Living

An independent living community is designed for people who can, and are, able to live independently but do not want to maintain a home with all of the home ownership responsibilities. In an Independent Living community there will most likely be people of the same age and interests. Most independent living communities offer activities and prepared meals along with a large array of amenities. There will be stimulating activities, educational trips, craft and painting classes, swimming, exercise and much more. The move to a good independent community can be a fairly smooth transition offering a lifestyle similar to living at home, with some very nice added advantages - no meals to cook, no yard work and little or no housecleaning.

More often than not the new resident is amazed at how much the new life style offers them more freedom, fewer worries and new opportunities.

Following the move into an independent community in San Diego, California, a new resident said to me, "I really wish I had done this sooner. Now I am free to do the things I really like to do... like read, play golf, dine out, and, practically all under the same roof. There are no weeds to be pulled, cooking to be done, or house to be cleaned. I come and go as I please and even have transportation when I need it. My children had encouraged me to do this five years ago but I said, "Pardon me, but I'm not ready yet."

"Now when I hear someone say those words my question to them is: 'not ready for what?' I have more freedom and independence now than I have had for the last 20 years because my time is my own, to do what I want to with it.

"My daughter who lives on the East Coast says she no longer feels guilty because she knows I am happy, not lonely, and in a safe place."

Sometimes it is hard to determine appropriate placement for a loved one. This is where creativity comes in and where a good marketing/community relations person can help to make a difference.

Thinking back to 1993 while working as a Marketing Director in a not-for profit assisted living/independent living community in San Diego, a particular resident and her family come to mind.

Lucy was a delightful woman who had been married for 65 years. Her husband who had retired from a 30-year career at a nearby university died suddenly and Lucy was left with a large home to care for.

While she loved her neighborhood, both Lucy and her daughter, Sheila, decided that some type of Senior Living Community would be a good option. Suffering from a past leg injury, Lucy depended upon a wheelchair to go any distance and because of that she was placed in assisted living. While working there, I had the opportunity to get to know Lucy, learn about her life experiences and meet some of her family.

A couple of years later when I made a career change to a continuing care community in Chula Vista, it was difficult to say good-bye to Lucy.

But as fate would have it, one day while in my new office I received a telephone call from Lucy's daughter, Sheila. She expressed concern about her mom's unhappiness in her current situation and wanted to know if there were any assisted living openings at the community in Chula Vista. I knew we had none. The assisted living apartments were 100% occupied and there was a waiting list of 30. Knowing this, I asked Sheila if her mom could walk with a walker. She said, "I don't know, but I will ask her." Sheila called me the following day and said her mom wanted to "graduate" to a walker and would start working with it right away. I said "great" and we made plans to reserve a one-bedroom apartment for her mom. Immediately I spoke to my Executive Director and told him about this wonderful resident with a walker who would be moving into an independent apartment. His response was positive and he was happy that we could help but he explained that she would not be able to take the walker into the dining room. I knew she couldn't go from the hall to the dining room without the assistance of her walker and I expressed this concern to him. He suggested that I ask her if she could use a cane. I called Sheila and apologetically asked if she thought her mom could possibly use a cane to ambulate to the dining room, even two canes if needed. Once again, she said, "I don't know but I will ask my mom." To shorten the story Lucy found that she could get along just fine with a four-pronged cane to make her way to the dining room and she would use a walker to get around in her apartment.

So as it worked out, Lucy was able to live much more independently than she was once told she could. While this would not be possible for everyone, it is important to know that there is usually more than one option.

Keep in mind, it is always best to select a community where independence is fostered.

Think for a minute about a tennis game. If you have played tennis you know that it is best to play with someone who plays better than you. It sharpens your skills and makes you a better player. The same can be said for living in a retirement community where independence is encouraged. I have seen residents live up to the level of independence expected of them and Lucy is a good example of the possibilities!

Lucy ended up moving from an assisted living studio apartment in a somewhat worn community where she depended upon a wheelchair to get around into a beautiful one-bedroom apartment in a lovely community where she was able to regain some of her independence, participate more in activities and have a better quality of life.

In 2004, I received a letter from Sheila announcing that Lucy had passed away. Thanking me again, Sheila wanted me to know what a difference the move had made in Lucy's final 10 years of life.

Assisted Living

Assisted Living Communities were once known as "old folks homes." They were often dark, dreary buildings with unpleasant odors throughout. Occupied wheelchairs and walkers were lined up against the wall at the entry-way. Sad looking occupants occupied those seats and you could often hear weeping and wailing. I remember a community in Hillcrest, California where I visited my friend's grandfather. There were residents sitting in the hallway as I entered the building begging me to take them home. It was very depressing and it reminded me of a warehouse of debilitated, unhappy, uncared-for individuals. If that is your image of assisted living as it was mine, you can BANISH the thought. We have come a long way and many of the Assisted Living Communities in the U.S. can be likened to country club living with upscale surroundings featuring luxury apartments and cottages.

Assisted Living is for people needing assistance with Activities of Daily Living (ADLs) but wish to live as independently as possible for as long as possible. Assisted Living serves as a bridge between independent living and nursing homes. ADLs such as eating, bathing, dressing, laundry, housekeeping, and assistance with medications are provided. Prior to moving into an Assisted Living Community a prospective resident is assessed and an appropriate level of care is determined. Some communities include the first level of care in the monthly rental amount. Residents are usually re-assessed on an ongoing basis to ensure that proper care is being given. Often residents improve and a lower level of care can be administered, creating more independence for the resident and lowering the cost, too. There should be a detailed daily plan for your loved one. This is a document that the staff is required to follow and fulfill and you are entitled to a copy of it. (This is a key issue - even though you have a copy of this schedule, it is a good idea to stop in when not expected to see if the care plan is being followed - more about this in Chapter Four, *Care Enough to Ask, Look and Do*). A Physician's Report and a complete list of medications will be required as part of the move-in procedure. If this is going to be a long-distance move, many times the staff in the community of your choice can get the appropriate paperwork and assessment from the out of town physician.

Assisted Living is not an alternative to nursing or memory care. However, some Assisted Living Communities do have memory care units for those suffering from Alzheimer's/dementia (look in the back of the book for a screening tool).

It should be noted that extra caution should be taken when considering an Assisted Living Community. While there are various levels of care offered, some folks will be at the highest level of care and in this case it may be necessary to stay on top of what care is actually being given.

The following is an account of a horrifying story that took place in a continuing care community in Southern California. The particular city is known for rat and rodent problems. The rats are known to chew through the PVC pipe in homes, invade and chew into sprinkler systems and just about any other place where it is dark and/or moist.

There was a couple (Mr. & Mrs. Corson) living in the assisted living wing of this particular community. They rated high on the level of care scale (see Chapter Seven, *Know How Care Levels are Determined*) but did not need memory care or skilled nursing.

It seems that some of the local rodents had found their way into this couple's apartment and had set up housekeeping. Nothing was known about this until one Saturday afternoon.

It was the weekend when many families visit their parents and loved ones. Mr. & Mrs. Corson were happy to see their daughter, Donna. Up until this time Donna had been very satisfied with the care being given to her parents. On this particular afternoon, Mrs. Corson complained that her toes hurt. When Donna pulled the covers back the sight of her mom's toes was both shocking and scary. The toes were raw as though something had been gnawing on them. Unfortunately, that is exactly what had been happening. Mr. & Mrs. Corson, seeing what appeared to be cute little mice in their apartment, decided to make pets out of them. Each night they would put crackers and small pieces of food under the covers at the foot of the bed for them to nibble on. Obviously the mice had found the snacks and Mrs. Corson's toes.

This was a blatant case of neglect and a lack of complying with a prescribed care plan. They were to be having two-hour room checks every day, 24 hours a day. Housekeeping was scheduled to be doing daily bed making and weekly housecleaning. Since the family members had been out of town for the past six weeks, the Corson's were charted to have help daily with dressing, grooming and bathing. None of these things were being done.

The County Health Department was called in, citations were given to the community and the assisted living section was closed down for further investigation.

This is a true story and hopefully something like this

does not happen to you. It is fair warning though. If you have loved ones living in a Senior Living Community keep in touch with them-visit often. If you can't be there, send a friend. You can never be too careful.

Skilled Nursing Facilities (SNF)

Skilled Nursing Facilities (SNF) and Nursing Homes are designed to care for very frail people who are not able to care for themselves and have numerous health care requirements. People in SNF and Nursing Homes are pretty much bed-bound and have an inability to ambulate on their own. Some nursing homes have memory care units where people with Alzheimer's and dementia can live comfortably.

Admission to a Skilled Nursing/dementia Facility is ordered by the physician.

Alzheimer's/ Memory Care/ Dementia

Some Skilled Nursing Communities have Memory Care Units where people with varying degrees of memory loss can be accommodated.

Assisted Living Communities sometimes work very well for people with dementia depending upon the level of dementia. This can be determined by the staff and the resident's physician.

A good Alzheimer's Unit is designed in a certain way for good reason. For instance, the floor should be simple, without complicated designs. Confusion takes place if there is too much variation in the floor coverings and the patient may be afraid to take a step. Shadows are confusing too. The lighting should be bright but not glaring. Noise level should be low to avoid agitation caused by loud noises. Residents' rooms should have identifiers such as large decals or a certain color to aid the resident in finding his room. Entry ways should be alarmed and locked in a true Alzheimer's unit. Hallways should all lead back to the same place to prevent the patient from getting lost. There should be plenty of space to walk. Staff should be available for residents who tend to wander at night or for those who have Sundowners Disease (Rupp, Joyce 1999).

Before admitting anyone to a dementia/Alzheimer's/ memory care unit, the physician must be consulted and a physicians report or History and Physical (H&P) is required by the admitting facility. Sometimes a psychological evaluation must be included in the admitting paperwork.

"Six-Packs"

An Adult Foster Care is basically the same as a Board and Care Community. These communities are small, usually found in a large home within a residential neighborhood. They typically have six bedrooms and have been nicknamed "six-packs." These are ideal for people who want a small, intimate, family-type atmosphere. Meals are served at a family style table where all residents eat together. There is usually a living room and TV room where residents gather. Many of these communities have a nurse on staff or on-call. The residents can enjoy activities and private transportation is provided for trips to the doctor and shopping. Legitimate Foster Care homes are licensed by the State and have strict regulations. Unlicensed homes do exist but are not recommended.

Continuing Care Communities (CCRC)

CCRCs combine independent living, assisted living and nursing care, and sometimes a memory care unit. Upon entrance to a CCRC you typically pay a large down-payment with sizeable monthly payments for your accommodations. When you buy into a CCRC you are assured that you will have care for the rest of your life. The down side is that in many of the CCRCs you can only receive a portion of your investment back should you decide that the community is not right for you. Bottom line is this - the longer you live in a CCRC the less of your investment you will receive back and at some point - determined by the particular community- none of your investment will be returned.

However, some folks want the security of knowing that no matter what, they can live in the chosen community for the rest of their life. It is also worth noting that a prospective resident must go through rigorous testing to be accepted into this type of community. An individual is required to have near perfect physical, mental and psychosocial health.

One couple I interviewed lived in a CCRC in Southern Oregon. After two years they moved out losing a portion of their investment. In talking with the wife, she said her husband's comment was " I don't want to go there and park my brain for the rest of my life." He felt he no longer had control of his own life. On the other hand the wife liked the social opportunities and luxurious lifestyle and said she would have been happy to stay.

Rental Communities

There are various types of rental communities for seniors. In some you are required to pay an entrance fee and make a commitment to a long-term lease. Others are on a month to month basis with a 30-day notice to vacate requirement. The attractive thing about a rental situation is that you are free to invest your money elsewhere and if the community doesn't suit you it is easy to move to a new location.

Senior apartment complexes cater to individuals 55 and over. There is a beautiful community of this type in Plano, Texas. It is a 55+ gated community, has beautiful landscaping, a pool, clubhouse, activities and limited meal service. This community is an exception to the rule when it comes to senior apartment living. The large customized apartments with patios, balconies and fireplaces are perfect for individuals who love to entertain but prefer not to do a lot of yard work and maintain large homes. I would highly recommend this community as an option to seniors who are very independent (See back of the book for a Report Card Request).

Unlike the above community, many senior living apartments are smaller, have minimal services and fewer amenities. They are often subsidized by the county or government. For those on a limited budget this is an excellent option. Due to their popularity there is typically a long waiting list. Some do have clubhouses and monthly activities for resident enjoyment. I have seen people wait as long as two years for a vacancy.

Independent Buy-in Communities

This is a special category that is often overlooked when researching senior living options. In this setting residents buy their home or condo and are free to sell to anyone within the age requirement listed in the bylaws. These communities usually do not look like a retirement community, rather more like an upscale neighborhood with manicured lawns and yards. A clubhouse, dining room and sometimes a putting green and pool are included. Activities are offered as well.

There is a very high-end community of this type in Ashland, Oregon, where the needs of gardeners and horticulturists are satisfied by offering large individual plots of gardening space. I have seen squash, tomatoes, green beans, herbs and various berries, as well as many beautiful flowers produced from these plots. Often the residents share their crops with their neighbors and at times some of the fresh produce has been served in the dining room.

Chapter Four
Care Enough to Ask, Look and Do

It's important to ask enough questions and look behind enough doors so that you can pass the "gut check" - that is - the point when you feel confident in the pit of your stomach, and you know you can trust people with what is precious to you.

- David W. Mills

Selecting the right senior living option can be tedious. But by taking the right steps in advance can result in a good decision.

Transition at any age is difficult. Moving one's belongings, changing neighborhoods, and saying goodbye to material things can be painful and unsettling, not to mention leaving long-time friends.

Sometimes just the thought of moving is very overwhelming - but it all starts with asking questions.

On the following pages you will find sample questions to ask when beginning your search.

41

Ask the Right Questions

Considering and following guidelines listed below you will be on your way to making a sound and educated decision.

First, we will look at what is probably the most important issue - food.

This will be the determining factor on which many will base their final decision (understandably so).

Food:
1. How many items are on the menu?

2. Does the menu include sugar free, fat free, or diabetic meals?

3. Are vegetarian meals available?

4. How many choices will you have at each meal?

5. How many meals are included in your monthly fee?

6. Do you have to pay for a full meal plan or is there an optional plan?

7. Are seats assigned for meals or is it open seating?

8. Can meals be delivered to my apartment and is there a charge?

9. Can I invite friends and family to dinner or lunch?

10. Is there a private dining room where I can entertain my family or other group?

11. Is there a nutritionist on staff?

Financial: There are many questions that will need to be asked to get the full financial picture. You will need to define exactly what services you are paying for and can expect to be delivered.

1. Ask for a financial statement

2. Does the community have a good relationship with other businesses in town and do they pay their bills in a timely manner?

3. What is the amount of the monthly rent or mortgage?

4. Is a deposit required and is it refundable?

5. Is there a move-in fee or initiation fee? (Always ask if this can be waived. Most marketing personnel have options that they can offer as move-in incentives.)

6. Is there a move-in special that you can take advantage of?

7. What exactly does the monthly fee include?

8. Are there rent increases? How often? How much?

9. Is it possible to pay a year or six months in advance to get a discounted rate? And how much would it be?

10. If it is an Assisted Living Community, does the monthly fee include levels of care (Please see Chapter 7, *Know How Care Levels are Determined*).

11. How much is each additional level of care and what is included?

11. If pets are allowed, is there a pet deposit and is any of it refundable?

12. Who manages the community? This is a very important question. By all means, if it is possible, select a community that is locally owned and managed. You stand a much better chance of getting what you are promised with local owners/managers. There is more staff accountability when owners are in the vicinity. It is my observation that communities managed by a group of professionals thousands of miles away suffer and become victims of "bottom line" priorities. Many times retirement homes are only a portion of the portfolio and purchased to be the money makers to support other interests. There are several retirement communities in Southern Oregon that fall into this category and when interviewing the residents you hear the same complaints over and over. "The community is short staffed... the food is poor quality... the staff doesn't care." Interviews with residents of locally owned and managed communities reveal for the most part that they get what they were promised.

"Humans must breathe, but corporations must make money," a quote by Alice Embree. It is important to bear in mind, though, there is not a perfect place anywhere! So, we strive to select the best by doing our homework. And that is why you are reading this book!

Medical: Many seniors relocate to be closer to medical facilities. Needs change as we age - what was an excellent living situation at one point in time may become impractical as we age. With this in mind the search begins for a place with good hospitals and doctors.

1. Are there good hospitals and physicians available in your area of consideration?

2. Do doctors in the area take new Medicare patients?

3. Are there medical specialists in the area that can meet your specific needs?

4. If you have long-term care coverage can it be used at the community of your choice?

5. Is there a physician on staff at the community (applies to Assisted Living)?

6. Is there a registered nurse (Assisted Living)?

7. If you are looking at Independent Living can you have in-home care if needed?

8. If you order your medications online or through the Veterans Administration can you continue to do that once you move in? Or, do you have to use the community's prescription plan?

9. At what level of care must you move out of the community, if at all?

10. If you are new to the area can they recommend a good doctor, dentist?

Safety:
1. Is there someone at the front desk or entrance at all times?

2. Are the doors locked after a certain hour each evening?

3. Are the exit doors alarmed (this would be important in Assisted Living or higher levels of care)

4. Is the housekeeping staff trained to check for opened and unlocked windows?

5. Are the housekeeping staff and other staff members trained to keep an eye open for stale food and trash left around the apartment?

6. Is there a neighborhood watch program or buddy system in the community?

A Sad, but True Story

A community in San Diego, which accommodates residents from a very independent status to those receiving assisted living, made a very serious mistake several years ago.

It was November, days were beautiful and nights were cool requiring a sweater, sometimes a warmer jacket. Around 4:00 P.M. one Tuesday afternoon Mr. Thompson went out for a walk as he did about three or four times a week. Wearing his yellow golf sweater and some lightweight slacks he snapped the leash to Samson's collar (his dog) and off they went. Heading down Sixth Avenue at a moderate pace, he walked alongside the view of beautiful St. James Park, down around Hawthorne Street, and turned right heading toward Harbor Blvd.

Since the clocks had been turned back for daylight savings time it was beginning to get a little dusk. Just before they began to cross over Fourth Avenue, Mr. Thompson noticing that his shoelace was untied, bent down to lace up and in doing so let go of the leash. Samson was "free at last" and took off running down toward Harbor Boulevard, and of course did not answer to his name when called. This was concerning because it was getting darker and it was hard for Mr. Thompson to run or even walk very fast. But he just had to get Samson back - so off he went down the hill.

Meanwhile back at the community, the tables were set and people were gathering to go into the dining room. A couple of people asked about the whereabouts of their friend but no one seemed to know anything. One lady asked the dining room manager if she knew if Mr. Thompson was gone for the day or out of town. The answer was "I don't know."

The next day, Wednesday, as is customary in most communities, the residents woke up to the smells of coffee and breakfast being cooked. Most were ready to enjoy some delicious food, another day of activities and time to visit with friends. Again it was noticed by a resident that Mr. Thompson was missing and she asked the Dining Room Manager if she knew anything. The answer was "No, I don't."

At 2:00 P.M. that day Sally, Mr. Thompson's daughter called his apartment but there was no answer. After trying several times over a two hour period, she decided to call the Executive Director of the Community. He said he had no idea where the resident was but most likely was participating in an activity or out for a walk.

Later that day Sally called the apartment again - still no answer. She tried to reach the Executive Director again hoping to have him check the apartment. He was not available so his secretary took a message. Becoming very concerned, Sally threw some clothes in her car and began the drive from San Francisco to San Diego (about a 12-hour drive).

Day Three, Thursday. Five A.M. Sally arrived in San Diego, still no Dad. Executive Director unavailable, night staff did not know Mr. Thompson was missing. Sally called the home of the Executive Director and got the message machine. "Where is my Dad?!" she shouted into the receiver. Becoming very distraught by this time, Sally called the Police Department to file a missing persons report.

Day Four, Friday - still no sign of Mr. Thompson's whereabouts.

Day Five, Saturday - Sally received a call from Police Department. Her Dad had been found laying in a gutter alongside Harbor Boulevard, Samson's leash wrapped around his wrist, the yellow golf sweater draped over his body for warmth, wallet missing, body badly bruised with apparent severe blow to head.

A very sad story. Had the staff been alert, properly trained and responsive to the needs of the residents - those whom they are paid to serve, this never would have happened. Sally had trusted the staff at this community in San Diego to take good care of her Dad.

As it should have, this story made the newspapers, the regional news channels and was met with horror by other adult children who had entrusted the care of their parents to the staff of this community.

There was a massive move-out, and the Executive Director was fired from his position the following week. And to my knowledge that community has not yet regained the good reputation they once enjoyed.

The key issue here is to ask all of the questions about security and safety. Find out if the dining room staff and housekeepers have been trained to notice if residents are not around and to be aware of their comings and goings. Do they report this to the Executive Director and is there follow-up? Has a plan of action been put in place when someone doesn't show up for meals? Who is watching your loved ones? If you are paying for these services they should be delivered, no questions asked.

<u>Comfort</u>: Some things are not necessary but make life a lot more comfortable. The more home-like your new situation can be the better quality of life you will enjoy. You will undoubtedly have your own list of wants, but here are some that might make a difference.

1. Are pets allowed?

2. Can you bring your own furniture?

3. Is transportation provided on a regular basis to doctors, shopping, etc? Is there on-demand transportation for individual requests?

4. Does the company bus or vehicle have a wheelchair lift?

5. Is there a beauty/barber shop on site?

6. How many hours does the activity director work and are there activities on the weekend?

7. Is there a chapel and/or Bible studies?

8. Is the Activity Director open to new ideas and requests of the residents?

In a community in southern Oregon one woman from New York decided to poll other residents to see if any were from her home state. In the process she met many folks who wanted to find people from their home state. This was the birth of the Homestate Club. They began to have a monthly dinner honoring a different state each time serving food specific to their region. The chef of that particular community is very flexible and loves to please the residents. (My favorite was the roast beef and Yorkshire Pudding ordered up by some folks from the state of Connecticut.) Sometimes this group would show slides and share "local lore." What started out to be one person's search for other New Yorkers has blossomed and served to meet the needs of approximately 50 other residents who are from various other locations.

9. Are there washer/dryer hookups in the apartments?

10. Do the apartments have patios/balconies?

Questions That May Not Be Answered: Over the years in the "general question" category the most common queries have been about race, religion and male/female ratio. I can understand why this would be important. It is comfortable to spend time with people "like" us. But since information about race, religion and age cannot be given out (due to Fair Housing laws) you can ask your questions in a different way and draw your own conclusions. Consider the following questions.

1. Do you celebrate the Holidays? If so which ones?

2. Do you have church services? Which denominations?

3. Approximately how many men participate in your activities? How many women participate?

4. Have you ever had a Rabbi do a service in this community?

5. Do you celebrate Hanukkah?

6. Is there a Spanish-Speaking service?

Additional Questions:

1. How "green" is this community? Do they recycle? Do the apartments have heat pumps?

2. Can I have housekeeping more than once a week? How much will it cost?

3. Can I hire a companion? Can he/she spend the night?

4. Can I tip the staff?

5. Are wheelchairs allowed in the dining room?

6. Does the community have fire drills?

7. Do I get a discount on my rent if I am away on vacation? (Most communities will not charge for the food while you are away.)

8. Do the apartments have pull-cords or emergency buttons?

9. Are the toilets "high bowl" for ease in sitting?

Look for Blind Spots

Think about blind spots at some roadway intersections. Many times because the visibility is not clear in all directions, accidents happen! This can be true in making your Senior Living Community selection, so it is time to really open your eyes and take a good, hard look! I learned the lesson the hard way when I accepted a position at a community in a California resort area.

My husband and I were excited about the prospect of relocating from Plano, Texas back to the West Coast where we had spent most of our lives. It was an October afternoon when we arrived. I was excited to be interviewed for a Marketing Position in this upscale community. As I entered the dimly lit building the second shift receptionist greeted me and notified the Executive Director, Nancy Bonham, that I had arrived.

We spent an hour discussing the various aspects and requirements of the position, after which her assistant gave me a brief tour of the building. He was somewhat apologetic about the carpeting and some other aspects of the building but mentioned that replacement of the carpeting was in the budget.

I was offered and accepted the position and it was

determined that I would become part of the staff the first
of January.

As I walked back to the car where my husband waited,
I had a slight sinking feeling but could not determine
why I felt that way. It did seem a little odd since I had
just landed the "job of my dreams." After discussing the
feeling with my husband, we both decided that I was
probably just tired from the flight and the stress and just
needed a good night's rest. The next day we caught our
flight back home to Texas. Over the next two months we
set our sights on the goal, sold our home, packed up, and
made our way back to California.

We have all heard the term "the honeymoon is over."
That was the case for me the first day on the job at the
new community. I arrived early, the day was bright,
drapes were pulled and guess what - all I could see were
glaring dirt spots on the carpeting in the lobby. The chairs
and couches, now exposed in the daylight, were soiled
and worn. As I made my way through the building that
day things only got worse. The air was stale or in some
cases, offensive. The dining room had mismatched dishes,
wrinkled tablecloths, and the wait staff had soiled uniforms. The story goes on and does not get better.

As weeks passed I became disappointed and concerned about the care given to residents. I questioned
my decision. Since we had moved lock-stock-and barrel,
there was no reversal possible at this point. I had to make
the best of the situation and hope for things to get better.
I stayed for one year, things did not get better. By far, the
most disheartening thing for me was that the residents
were not getting the services and amenities that they were

paying for. Many promises were made that things would get better by the owner who lived about 3,000 miles away. This was a good example of a community owned and operated by absentee owners who rarely visited and whose only interest was the bottom line. The company went into bankruptcy two years later.

That was a hard year for me and much of it was spent anguishing over my naiveté. In my excitement for a new adventure I was blinded to the reality of the situation and had to live with it. My caution to you is to keep your eyes wide open. Look at the apartments, common areas and outside areas at different times of the day.

1. Notice the entryway to the building. Is it clean and neat?

2. Is the room cheerful and light as you enter the building?

3. Look Down! Are the carpets clean?

4. Sniff! Are there unpleasant odors? (If your sense of smell isn't great bring a friend who has a good sniffer.)

5. Are there residents sleeping in the lobby?

6. Does the staff greet you in a pleasant manner?

7. Are the staff members dressed neatly?

8. Look at the dining room, is there food on the floor? Are the carpets badly spotted?

9. Are the tablecloths wrinkled or spotted?

10. If the tables have glass tops are they smudged and unclean?

11. Are the hallways and door openings wide enough to accommodate wheelchairs and walkers?

12. Are there ample common areas for residents to spend time in? Examples would be lounges on each floor, library, fireside with chairs, activity room, exercise room.

13. Is there an area outside where residents can walk or sit when weather permits?

14. Is there a designated area for dogs and a place to walk them (if permitted)?

15. Is the public restroom clean and stocked with the necessary items?

16. Are there dirt marks and smudges on the walls?

After taking a good hard look at the community, there are some action items for you to do to further your search.

Action Items:
1. Visit at odd times, late at night and on weekends. How many staff members are working?

2. Interview a resident. Ask how long they have lived in the community-what are their likes and dislikes. Interview more than one resident.

3. Make an appointment with the Administrator. Ask how long she has been on the job. Try to get a general idea of her philosophy about working for older people.

4. Try meals at different times of the day on several different occasions.

5. Sit in on an activity.

6. Call the community to see how the telephone is answered. What response do you get to your inquiry?

7. Do a Google search on the community to see if there has been any negative press.

8. Arrange for your mom to stay overnight. Most communities have guest apartments and will allow prospective residents to stay free for a couple of nights. It is a good way to test the waters, learn about the other residents, taste the food and see how the community operates.

Selecting the right "new home" is done by taking a series of small steps. Once you have carefully researched all areas and begin to feel confident that you have a good understanding of what to expect, you are approaching the final decision stage. But, just a few more cautions. There are possible obstacles that you will want to be aware of.

Chapter 5 covers some of those obstacles and will give you a head start on what you might expect as you go through the selection process.

Chapter Five
Know the Obstacles

If you find a path with no obstacles, it probably doesn't lead anywhere.

-Frank A. Clark

How important is the interview? Following is part of an interview that took place in a community in Rancho Mirage, California in 2001. The names are fictitious but the conversation went something like this:

Participating in this interview were Mr. & Mrs. Lawson, Sharon Smith - their daughter, and Carol Anderson - the Marketing Director of the community.

Carol: Good afternoon, I am Carol. Welcome to Happy Acres!

M/M Lawson: *Hello.*

Sharon Smith: *Hi, I am the one who talked to you earlier this week. Mom and Dad really need to move to a community but are a little hesitant. My sister called too but she couldn't be here today.*

Carol: Okay, well let's go over here to my office and we can talk a little, then if you would like we can take a little tour.

Can I offer you something to drink, coffee, tea, water or maybe some lemonade?

Sharon Smith: *Mom shouldn't have coffee and nothing with sugar for Dad. So I would say we won't have anything right now.*

Carol: Thank you so much for coming in. Have a seat and please make yourself comfortable. I hope we weren't too difficult to find.

Sharon Smith: *No, you were easy to find. My parents just weren't ready on time, then we ran into traffic so it made us a little late. I told them we had an appointment at 10:00 but I can only do so much.*

Carol: No problem. Mr. and Mrs. Lawson, how are you both doing today? You both look so nice.

Sharon Smith: *Well, they usually get dressed up on Sunday for church but I told them they needed to look very nice for this meeting with you. Daddy doesn't shave some days and often wears the same shirt for a week at a time. Mom usually has her hair done once a week but it usually looks pretty messy by the 5th day, but I got them over here so that is what counts.*

Carol: Well Mr. & Mrs. Lawson, tell me a little about yourselves. Where do you live now and maybe a little about how I might answer some questions you have about Happy Acres.

Mrs. Lawson: *Well, I...*

Sharon Smith: *Mom and Dad live on Idaho Street and have lived there for 43 years. I don't know if they really have questions - it is more a case of me and my sister thinking they should be where they get some help. We both work and do not have time to clean and* *cook for them, let alone take care of the yard. And, stuff! You should see the stuff! I think mom and dad have things from the day they moved into the house. I don't know how they find anything.*

Carol: Mr. Lawson, what did you do in your career?

Mr. Lawson: *I was a CPA.*

Sharon Smith: Yes, Daddy was a CPA, but he really cannot even handle the checkbook at this point and that is one of the reasons I think they need to make some changes.

Carol: Mrs. Lawson, what are some of the things you like to do during the day? We have lots of interesting activities, classes and events that might interest you, both of you for that matter.

Mrs. Lawson: *Well....*

Sharon Smith: *That's the problem, my parents don't like to do much of anything. I just can't be there for them all of the time.*

Carol: Mrs. Lawson, I like your pin with a dog on it. Do you like dogs? Do you have a dog or cat?

Sharon Smith: *That's another thing, mom and dad have a dachshund but I think they should get rid of it.*

Carol: Happy Acres is a pet-friendly community and we even have folks here who will walk your dog for you. We have a dog run on the west side of the property too.

Mr. Lawson: *Would we be able to bring our dog then?*

Sharon Smith: *Now, Dad, I don't think that is a good idea. We need to make your life as simple as possible. You and mom are getting on in years you know.*

The conversation got worse!

What was wrong with this interview?

As you can see Sharon monopolized the conversation, and in the process belittled and "children-ized" her parents. Carol, the Marketing Director was trying to draw them out, to find out a little about them. Sharon answered for her parents as though they weren't even in the room. She did not give them a chance to express themselves. She brought negativity to the table. True, Mr. & Mrs. Lawson may be elderly and cannot get around as well, but they can still think, have an opinion and can lead a productive life and they matter!

This does not represent a good beginning to making a life changing decision. It is true that adult children do, at some point, become "the parent," but it must be handled with gentleness and care. A good book to read on role for adult children is *When Roles Reverse: A Guide to Parenting Your Parents* by Jim Comer (see bibliography).

MORE OBSTACLES

Pardon Me, but I'm Not Ready Yet!

This is probably the most common statement heard by adult children when they begin to suggest that their parents need to look at some type of senior living accommodations.

One way to combat this problem is to start the conversation long before the need ever arises. Get your loved ones use to the idea beforehand. If you find you are in a situation where the move needs to be imminent - here are some suggestions.

Look at safety issues- are your loved ones safe living alone in their home? Do they have falls? Are they still driving? Parents keep children safe when they know they are in danger - you must become the "parent" at this time in order to keep them safe (Comer, Jim 2006).

Shop on your own. Select a couple of good communities and then schedule a time for you and your loved ones to visit together.

Get References ahead of time from friends, doctors and senior centers.

Once you have identified the right community ask the Administrator or Director of Community Relations to assist you in helping your loved ones to see the need for a move. Have one of them call and invite your parents to lunch.

Contact friends who have helped their parents transition to retirement living. Learn of their successes - failures. The old saying "two heads are better than one," definitely applies here.

They feel that they cannot afford it.

Today's prices sound like a huge sum of money compared to years ago when they were looking for a new place to live. This is where you emphasize the abundance of amenities that are included in the rent. New friends and the security of always having someone around in case of emergency is another important plus.

Parents sometimes resent adult children taking over.

A common obstacle are feelings of resentment towards family members. Mom feels "after all she has been making her own decisions for 80 years, why does it need to stop now and who does she (her daughter) think she is?" (Comer, Jim 2006).

I Don't Want to Leave My Pet!

There is an easy solution to this one. Find a community where pets are welcome. I visited one community in Carlsbad, California where there was a resident dog. He was cared for by the staff and felt comfortable roaming the community at will. Another community had an aviary with many colorful birds and exotic plants. Natural surroundings are life-giving at any age.

Intergenerational activities are good too. Some communities have regular interaction with local schools. An excellent book on this idea is *The Eden Alternative* by William H. Thomas. He addresses the value of incorporating animals, and all of nature into the lives of seniors living in an institution. Most communities allow residents to have small dogs and cats.

Will This be the Last Place I Live?

This can be a dreary thought and for all practical purposes may be true. However the focus can be placed on the many advantages of the new home and the new friends and activities. I heard an enlightening conversation between a friend and his neighbor recently. The neighbor was in a position where he needed to move to an Assisted Living Community and was not happy about it. He felt as though he was giving up all of his independence and his lifetime of accumulations and accomplishments. The friend said, "Well, you know my wife and I are probably going to do this in the near future but we kind of look at it as another new adventure." The neighbor then said, "I had never looked at it that way."

Will I be accepted, will I make friends? Will my wardrobe be acceptable? Are there cliques?

Unfortunately these thoughts are just as real at age 80 as they are in Junior High School. It is like the "new kid on the block" jitters.

Most communities have a staff member or volunteer who will take a new resident under their wing to help them to assimilate into the community. If they don't there are usually residents that like to befriend new people. One community I worked in had a group of 15 residents called "The Friends." They each took turns coming alongside new neighbors to help them in adjusting.

DENIAL

Denial-Adult Children

Number one obstacle for adult children and caregivers is denial. Adult children, in particular, do not want to believe that their loved ones are changing, maybe failing and need help. The comment most often heard is "Oh, mom is just a little forgetful." While this may be true, there may be more to it. Maybe mom is leaving things on the stove too long. Maybe mom is forgetting to lock her door at night. Maybe mom is getting lost when she drives to the grocery store. Maybe mom is very depressed and lonely but just doesn't show it when family is around.

Picturing our loved ones as they use to be is not easily erased from our way of thinking. We want to think of them as capable, healthy and wise as they once were. They may still have some of these attributes but for family and those emotionally involved it is hard to be objective.

While denial on the part of the adult child can delay mom or dad's move to senior living, studies show that most parents adjust to their new situation quickly. I have seen families standing in awe of the new life their parents have found. I heard one daughter say "I invited my mom to go out to lunch and shopping afterward. She had to cut our visit short because she and Dad had an afternoon bridge game with some new friends."

DENIAL

Parents or Other Loved One

Your parents or other loved ones may feel that they are "not ready," when in reality they should not be living alone, driving or continuing to assume the responsibilities and care of a home. They may not want to give up their "independence," not realizing that they will probably be gaining independence by giving up some of their responsibilities and will have more time to do the things they enjoy.

GUILT

Guilt-Adult Child

"How can I put my mom/dad in an institution? I should be taking care of her/him. I would probably never be forgiven if I even thought of doing it."

This is a very normal feeling and you may experience it. Just as a word of encouragement, I have seen and talked with hundreds of families going through this process and nine times out of ten, the guilt goes away once the loved one is adjusted in their new surroundings.

I received a call early one Monday morning from Sally Johnson, who is a partner in a very large law firm in New York. Sally had arrived in Oregon over the weekend to spend time with her parents. Seeing them for the first time after eight months time she was shocked at how much they had aged and she was very concerned that their safety was at risk. We met later that morning and as we talked I sensed Sally's deep feelings of guilt over not being able to care for her parents. Her career and a young family had to take precedence and she knew she had to make some hard decisions. Sally felt that she was betraying her parents by even suggesting an Assisted Living Community. Their resistance to the idea added to the deep burden she felt. With tearful eyes and a breaking heart, she said: "After all, my parents took care of me for 45 years and now I can't take care of them."

I suggested contacting the Jansen's physician about their situation. It turned out, in his professional opinion, the Jansen's needed to be in an environment where they could get some help with their Activities of Daily Living. He also felt they were unsafe living alone and that their diet needed improvement. Moving to an Independent Living community would be a solution but an Assisted Living Community would be ideal.

Sally and I met with our Director of Nursing and we agreed to set a date for Mr. & Mrs. Jansen to come in for lunch and a tour. It took some convincing on Sally's part to even get them to visit, but once they came to see us it seemed that they suddenly decided it would be a good idea. Two months later her parents moved into a two bedroom apartment in Assisted Living. And, their little dog came too. Mrs. Jansen made friends immediately and assimilated into her new lifestyle with ease. Mr. Jansen moved more slowly, but he did say to me one day, "It sure is nice not to worry about my yard."

Ultimately, Sally said goodbye to her guilt feelings, mom and dad found a new home that worked out pretty well for them.

Guilt-Parents or Other Loved Ones

It is usually after the move takes place that the adult children or other family members hear about how their parents felt guilty for years - they felt guilty about having their children worry about them. This is the case particularly when parents and children are separated by thousands of miles and at certain times it has been necessary to leave jobs, family and other responsibilities to attend to parents who have suddenly become ill, taken a fall or any other crisis situation.

DEPRESSION

Depression- Adult Child

I helped a brother and sister get their Dad situated in a beautiful one-bedroom apartment in a Independent/Assisted Living Community in Ashland, Oregon. Their mom had passed away two years prior after a long bout with cancer. Dad had been living alone in the family home with all of the memories of his wife, their happy marriage, and all of the years of child rearing. It seemed he had been a little depressed lately. During a family meeting the subject of a retirement community was discussed. Dad made the decision to seek us out on his own sometime after this meeting. After looking, Dad made plans to move into a one bedroom apartment. Following the decision, the daughter visited with me in my office on several occasions. The box of Kleenex came in handy more than once. She said she felt she was saying good-bye not only to her girlhood home, but to her parents life as she knew it. In one way she was very happy for him but was feeling a variety of emotions: depression, fear of the unknown, loss and a deep yearning for the way things use to be.

She visited the community often after her Dad moved in. Her Dad fit right in and felt very comfortable early on. Much to the children's surprise, Dad became very popular, very quickly (there is a high female to male ratio in most communities).

Depression-Parents

Most depression in the parents or loved ones stems from leaving behind all that was familiar. Often the move is made across country and good-byes are said to long-time friends, church families, and other social contacts.

GRIEVING

Adult Child & Parents-Grieving

Most residents and their families go through a grieving process - even though this is probably a healthy step, the detachment phase takes time. This loss may be real or perceived. Nonetheless, it is a change, goodbyes have been said to places, friends and all things familiar. The grieving process has been set in motion.

DABDA (denial, anger, bargaining, depression and acceptance) are common stages of grieving. While these feelings may not occur in any particular order they will most likely at some point arise. Just knowing that these feelings will play a part in this transition can ease the process.

Stuff & Things

One of the challenges when making this transition is deciding what to do with the stuff! There are many ways to downsize. One thing that works well is to help your loved one make a list. The only way to be objective with this is go to a room or location where you cannot see all of your stuff. Take a piece of paper, draw a line down the middle. On one side put NEEDS and on the other WANTS. This takes some thought because we often think our wants are our needs. A good way to look at needs is what do I actually use on a daily basis. (It can be a surprisingly few things.)

NEEDS	_WANTS_
Dresser	Wicker Love Seat
Bed	Antique Book Collection
Sofa	Grandfather Clock
End Tables	Elephant Statue
T.V.	Birdbath

This may take a few tries, but it seems to bring objectivity to the decision. You will probably find that your "needs" column is larger than your "wants" column. The secret is to taking as many of your "needs" with you and a few of your "wants."

If a person is just not ready to dispose of, give away or sell a lot of things, renting space in a local storage unit is helpful. This allows for time to decide what really fits into the new home. It is also a good way to see what you can live with or without.

Often people give some of their special items to family members or friends to keep for them. This does two things: 1) eliminates the sadness of giving everything away, and, 2) provides opportunities to see those things again.

There are many good estate sale experts available to help if you do decide to have a sale. Something new in the past few years is the Senior Move Manager. The individual holding this certificate has been specially trained to help folks decide what to bring and what to leave when downsizing. There are also Real Estate Agents who have been trained to work with seniors. They are called Senior Real Estate Agents.

Many retirement communities have an individual on staff who will help with your move. This person, the Move-in Coordinator, will even come to your home to help with what will fit into your new home. She will get down to the last detail with you on where to hang your pictures and what color throw pillows to use. If you need to sell your home she will help you to stage it for a successful sale.

This move can be such a positive opportunity for a resident who has lived alone for a long time in the same surroundings. It is not uncommon for residents to go out and buy all new furniture. Life takes on a leisurely air when someone else has to worry about cooking, cleaning, and yard work. Rather than waking up to "have-to's," it is a matter of choosing from a variety of enjoyable things to do.

Surprise, New Life!

I have seen it! Yes, people in their 70's, 80's and 90's can, and do, fall in love. I have sensed "love in the air" and witnessed many budding romances over my 25-year career in retirement communities. It was once said that an 80-year old woman still feels like the 18-year old girl who walked down the aisle long ago. I have attended more than a dozen wedding ceremonies throughout my career in retirement communities. Not to say that your single mom or dad will take this step, but they will make new friends and have new experiences. It is true that most communities have a high female to male ratio, but the men are not usually opposed to the extra pool of attention available to them.

Not only can a Senior Living Community bring a better quality of life for residents but many are willing to try things never before attempted. The new relaxed lifestyle, with little or no responsibility, tends to free people up. Ballroom dancing, tai chi, exercise classes, book clubs, etc., may be among the offerings.

Each family will have it's own unique set of circumstances and challenges. While this transition will probably be a bittersweet experience, it is important to remember that as time passes everyone will become accustomed to the new lifestyle.

Chapter Six
Carefully Plan the Move

The shortest answer is doing.

-English Proverb

The preliminary steps to be taken prior to moving day may take a period of months or years. If it is a need based transition the move may happen within two weeks. Consider the playwright. He dreams up the plot, develops the characters, does background research in the area or region, then writes the play. The hard part is done. Now it is time for the action to begin - the playwright may or may not be a part of the performance. In the end if the right questions have been asked and all of the research has been done, the play will be a success. The same can be said for your situation if you have done your homework, asked all of the questions, and looked at every aspect of the community. You are about ready for performance time and the play is about to begin!

An orderly systematic move will take a lot of the distress out of the move. A good moving checklist should be used. The following moving checklist itemizes the necessary steps before the actual move-in can take place.

Moving Checklist

❑ SET A MOVE-IN DATE

❑ SIGN PAPERWORK

❑ GIVE NOTICE AT CURRENT COMMUNITY

❑ GET PHYSICIANS REPORT AND
   MEDICATION LIST BACK TO NEW
   COMMUNITY

❑ DECIDE HOW MUCH DOWNSIZING HAS
   TO BE DONE-HIRE SOMEONE TO HELP IF
   NEEDED.

❑ CONTACT MOVER

❑ MOVING DAY KEEP MOM AND/OR DAD
   BUSY SO THEY DON'T HAVE TO BE
   CONCERNED WITH THE MOVE

Something helpful to do prior to moving day is pre-arrange with the community staff for mom or dad to have breakfast in their new home. That way they can spend time with their new neighbors and don't have to be concerned with the logistics of the move. While they are relaxing you or another helper can get everything set up and ready to go.

Once everything is moved in and turned on it is time for the celebration!

Put some fresh flowers on the table and maybe invite a few friends to have a "welcome home" party. Now mom and dad can begin to enjoy their new life and first day in the new apartment.

It may be that mom or dad are wary about staying alone for the first night or so. If this is the case you can stay to ease them into their surroundings. Think back about how you felt when you went to your first day of school. Were you nervous? Did you wonder what it would be like? Did you wonder if anyone would talk to you? Your Parent(s) may have some of these feelings. Be sensitive and be patient. You have come a long way and the hardest part of this process is about finished.

Chapter Seven
Know How Care Levels are Determined

It pays to plan ahead. It wasn't raining when Noah built the ark.

-Author Unknown

Following is a typical evaluation tool used to determine the appropriate level of care when considering Independent Living, Assisted Living or Nursing Care. Each community will differ somewhat on determination of cost and what is included in each level.

MOBILITY*

Moves about independently. Able to seek and follow directions. Able to evacuate building independently in case of emergency.   (1 point)

Ambulates with cane or walker. Moves about independently with wheelchair but needs help in case of emergency.   (2 points)

Requires occasional assistance to move about, but usually independent. (3 points)

Mobile but requires assistance in moving about due to confusion, limited vision or weakness. (4 points)

Assist in transfer to and from bed, chair or toilet. (5 points)

Requires transfer and transport assistance. Requires turning in bed and in wheelchair. Probably needs a Skilled Nursing Facility. (6 points)

* The rule of thumb for Assisted Living Communities is that the resident must be able to stand, pivot, and transfer with little or no assistance.

NUTRITION

Able to prepare own meals, eats without assistance. (1 point)

Can do some meal preparation, but needs main meal prepared daily. (3 points)

Needs all meals prepared and served. (4 points)

Needs assistance with eating, opening cartons, cutting food. (5 points)

Needs reminders to eat and assistance when eating.
Probably needs a Skilled Nursing Facility.   (6 points)

HYGIENE

Independent in all care including bathing, shaving,
dressing.   (1 point)

May require assistance, reminders or initiation assistance
with hygiene.   (4 points)

Dependent upon others for all personal hygiene.
                                                   (6 points)

HOUSEKEEPING

Independent in performing housekeeping functions
including bed making, vacuuming, cleaning and laundry.
                                                   (1 point)

May need assistance with heavy housekeeping,
vacuuming, laundry, changing linens.   (2 points)

Needs laundry and housekeeping services provided.
                                                   (3 points)

DRESSING

Independent and dresses appropriately.   (1 point)

Requires assistance with shoelaces, zippers, medical appliances or garments, or may require reminders.

(4 points)

Dependent upon others for dressing.   (5 points)

TOILETING

Independent and completely continent.   (1 point)

Incontinence, colostomy or catheter but is independent in self care.   (2 points)

Occasional problems with incontinence, colostomy or catheter care.   (4 points)

Cannot manage incontinence or may require physical assistance with toileting on a regular basis.   (5 points)

Regularly and uncontrollable incontinence or unable to communicate needs.   (6 points)

MEDICATION**

Responsible for self administration of medications.

(1 point)

Able to self-administer medications, but needs reminders and monitoring of process.   (3 points)

Family or home health agency administers medications.

(4 points)

Cannot administer own medications. Medications must be administered by licensed personnel.   (6 points)

** States Regulations vary regarding administration and storage of medications. It is necessary to check the state regulations for the community you are considering.

MENTAL STATUS

Oriented to person, place and time. Memory intact with occasional forgetfulness with no pattern of memory loss. Able to reason, plan and organize daily events. Can identify environmental needs and meet those needs.

(1 point)

Orientation to person, place and time may be minimally impaired. Requires occasional direction or guidance when getting from place to place. May have occasional confusion causing anxiety, withdrawal or depression.

(3 points)

Poor judgment. May require strong orientation assistance and reminders. (5 points)

Disoriented to time, place and person, or memory is severely impaired. Unable to follow directions. Probably needs a memory care facility. (6 points)

BEHAVIORAL STATUS

Copes well with inner stress, deals appropriately with emotions and deals appropriately with others. (1 point)

Periodic intervention from others to facilitate expression of emotions or periodic outbursts of anxiety or agitation.

(5 points)

Maximum intervention is required to manage behavior. May cause danger to self or others or is abusive or extremely uncooperative. (6 points)

INTERPRETATION

It is important to remember that all communities are different and have their own method of evaluating residents. On the following page you will find guidelines that will give you a general idea of appropriate placement for your loved one. There are gray areas and many times placement is open for interpretation by staff conducting the interview. It should also be noted that a resident's scores may change on different days according to health status and medication. This needs to be discussed with the physician.

Now go through each section, add up the totals and check against the following grid. TOTAL: _____ __

SCORES

34-50:   Residents of Nursing Homes****

19-40:   Residents of Assisted Living Facilities

13-23:   Residents of Congregate Senior Housing Communities/ Supportive Housing

8-18:   Residents of Independent Living/ Senior Apartments

***If a candidate scores a 6 in any category, probably the most appropriate level of care will probably be a specially equipped assisted living facility or a nursing home.

Chapter Eight
The Ideal Home

Mid pleasures and places though we may roam, be it ever so humble, there's no place like home.

- John Howard Payne

One sunny Tuesday morning in Southern Oregon, mom and I, after a tasty breakfast, decided to drop in on some of the retirement communities in the area. I had broached the subject over the past year, we had visited a few places, but mom wasn't real excited about it. To my surprise, on this particular day she thought it would be a good idea.

As we drove up to one Medford retirement community we were aware of the beautiful hanging baskets in the Porte Cache. There were lots of other shrubs and flowering plants around the front of the building too. After parking and as we walked into the bright and cheerful building, we were greeted by a very friendly, neatly dressed receptionist. My eyes spanned across the lobby to the expansive windows facing the courtyard. We saw fountains, waterways and beautiful flowering plants.

The Community Relations Director (CRD) came
out immediately and greeted us warmly. As we talked we
explained the reason for our visit. Most of the conversation was spent letting my mom express her thoughts. I
was happy she felt so comfortable with sharing her feelings. The General Manager soon came by and introduced
himself and offered to answer any questions we might
have.

The next step was to look at the common areas and
some of the apartments. We noticed many areas where a
resident could visit with friends, a library, a beautiful spa-
cious dining room, a bistro and a room called the Courtyard Hall with an inviting dance floor. There was also a
beauty shop, computer room, theater lounge and a gift
shop.

The apartments were large and airy, had walk-in
closets, in-room emergency call buttons, individually
controlled heating and air, walk-in showers and some had
washer dryer hookups.

We also noticed the attractive handrails in the hallways which were useful, but decorative. There was good
lighting with chairs spaced purposefully along the way for
rest stops.

We noted that there was a community bus which was
equipped with a wheelchair lift. Residents signed a roster
for the various trips offered throughout the week. The bus
is also used for day and overnight trips to events and various locations.

This particular community not only had Independent
Living Apartments but 16 dedicated personal care apartments where residents can have assistance with bathing,

grooming, dressing and medication reminders. The Registered Nurse (RN) on staff manages this area of the building.

As we toured the rest of the community we noticed that everything was sparkling clean, carpets were without spots, there were no unpleasant odors.

We were invited to and accepted a lunch invitation that day. The dining room had neatly appointed tables each with fresh flowers. The wait staff were crisply dressed and attentive to the residents. The menu had about 65 items from which to choose along with a daily special. The food was attractively presented and served in a timely manner. Hot items were hot and everything was fresh and delicious.

After lunch there was an activity in the garden room. A local author was bringing her books and doing a reading and book signing. We decided to stay (since Mom is a retired librarian). It was a good opportunity to sample an event and meet some of the residents. We heard that some of the other residents were out on a day trip to nearby Emigrant Lake, boating, fishing and picnicking, one of the popular recurring events offered to the residents.

At about 2:00 we were tired and felt satisfied that we had learned a lot about the community. There was no pressure from the CRD. She invited us to come back whenever we felt like it and gave us some information to look over and ask questions at a future time.

Mom and I felt good about this community. The general feeling we got when we walked in the door, the cleanliness of the building and the feeling that the residents come first, were all qualities we felt we wanted in a community. While we were not ready at that point to make a commitment, we did feel we would like to go back for another visit.

Long story shortened, we did visit three more times. After doing our homework we felt secure in putting mom on the VIP list. There was a fully refundable deposit required at that time and we told the CRD exactly the type of apartment we would be interested in. This also entitled me and my mom to lunch or dinner once a week until she moved in, monthly newsletters and an open invitation to attend all activities. Four months later the "perfect" apartment became available and mom moved in. She has been living in that community for three years now and has never regretted her move. Doing the homework first and having the option of waiting for the right situation paid off!

See Report Card Requests in the back of the book.

Chapter Nine
Know Your Resources (Annotated Bibliography)

There is no end to the adventure that we can have if only we seek them with our eyes open.

- Jawaharlal Nehru

The following is a list of helpful resources.

Beck, Alan M., Katcher, Arron; Marshall-Thomas, Elizabeth. (1996) Between Pets and People. Purdue Press., Purdue, PA

Discussion about the importance of animal companionship. Documented test results of a 1992 study showed that lower blood pressure and lower blood fat levels appeared in pet owners. Also covers material on pet therapy and how we can learn from pets.

Comer, Jim, (2006). When Roles Reverse: A Guide to Parenting Your Parents, Hampton Roads Publishing Co., Charlottesville, VA

What do you do with 55 years of accumulated personal items, real estate, finances, automobiles? This publication covers these practical areas as well as what to do about Medicaid, Medicare, Long Term Care Insurance, Veterans Benefits and all other types of assistance. Websites and telephone numbers are included for Agencies on Aging along with a questionnaire to assist adult children when they suddenly have to become the parent.

Genovese, Rosalie G., Americans at Midlife-Caught between Generations. Bergin & Garvey (1997) Westport, CT.

Americans at Midlife is a book about the middle years, with chapters on such issues as the not-so-empty nest and "boomerang kids," relationships with aging parents, the special concerns of midlife women, and work and retirement planning.

Hall, Julie. (2008) Boomer Burden: Dealing with Your Parents' Lifetime Accumulation of Stuff. Thomas Nelson. Nashville, TN.

Estate liquidator Julie Hall shows Baby Boomers how to deal with the challenge of dividing the accumulated wealth and property of their loved one's when suddenly the adult child is in charge. Suggest what to do with the stuff, who to get help from and suggest practical ways to go through the process.

Hutchinson, Joyce, Rupp, Joyce. (1999) May I Walk You Home. Ave Maria Press. Notre Dame, Indiana.

Joyce Hutchinson and Joyce Rupp capture the spirit of that person companionship for those who accompany the dying on their final journey. Hutchinson's moving stories relate her many experiences of caring for the dying, tracing the moments of joy, experiences of connection, and glimpses of heaven that occur along the way. Rupp's simple and tender prayers express beautifully the struggle and rewards of this companionship, offering caregivers both strength and hope.

Jacobs, Barry J., (2006) The Caregivers Survival Guide: Looking After Yourself and Your Family While Helping an Aging Parent. Guilford Publications. New York, NY.

The authors capture the spirit of those who accompany loved ones who are in their final days. An encouraging and inspirational work appropriate for family members, caregivers, pastors or those in the healthcare field.

Mace, Nancy L., Rabins, Peter (2001). 36-Hour Day Baltimore, MD: Johns Hopkins Publishing Co.

This is a Family Guide to Caring for People with Alzheimer Disease, other dementias, and memory loss in later life.

Thomas, William H., (1996) Eden Alternative, The: Nature, Hope & Nursing Homes, Acton, MA: Vanderwyk and Burnham

This is a account of a different approach to life for the elderly called the Eden Alternative. It covers how a community in New York incorporated plants, birds, dogs, cats and gardens into the daily life of and living accommodations of 80 residents. There was also a day care center and an after school program to bring a multi-generational aspect to the community.

The benefits and lasting impact of this type of environment are discussed.

Simpkins, Daphne. (2003) The Long Good Night: My Father's Journey into Alzheimer's. Eerdmans, William B. Publishing Company. Grand Rapids, MI.

In "The Long Good Night" Daphne Simpkins chronicles the slow, sometimes heartbreaking decline of her father from the disease, but also contradicts the prevailing opinion that caregivers can experience only suffering and chaos during this difficult season.

Chapter Ten

Know the Terms (Glossary)

In three words I can sum up everything I've learned about life: it goes on.

- Robert Frost

The following is a list of terms you may need:

ADLs: Activities of Daily Living. Activities such as bathing, grooming, dressing, eating.

AGING IN PLACE: The concept of a resident remaining in his/her living environment in the event of physical and mental caused by the aging process.

CARE PLAN: A prescribed plan of care for an assisted living or nursing home resident.

CHILDREN-IZE (my own term): to talk down to, treat like a child, and patronize an elderly person.

CCRC: Continuing Care Retirement Community. Housing community that provides a continuum of care for seniors, including independent living, assisted living, nursing care, Alzheimer's and memory care.

CRD: Community Relations Director-Marketing and sales.

DEMENTIA: A progressive neurological or cognitive disorder that affects memory and judgment.

DON: Director of Nursing

EXTENDED CARE: Could mean assisted living, could mean memory care, could mean skilled nursing or rehab.

H&P: History and Physical

HOME HEALTH CARE: Medical and nursing care provided for resident in his/her own home.

HOSPICE CARE: Care provided to those with a terminal illness. Most hospice care is provided in the resident's home.

LEVELS OF CARE: A grid which determines the care needed by a resident. The resident's level of ability is graded based on how much care is needed and they are charged accordingly.

NON AMBULATORY: Inability to walk, usually bedridden.

RN: Registered Nurse.

REHAB: Rehabilitation services. Could be occupational therapy. Could be physical therapy. Often rehabilitation facilities are temporary stay locations for people who have had a recent hospital stay.

RESPITE CARE: A temporary accommodation available for those recovering from an illness. Usually found in an assisted living facility.

SIX PACK: A privately owned adult foster care or board and care home consisting of approximately six bedrooms.

SNF: Skilled Nursing Facility

Chapter Eleven
Sample Report Card

The greatest of faults, I should say, is to be conscious of none.

- Thomas Carlyle

The following is a sample form of a request for a Report Card:

Name of Community: *Otter View Landing*

Type of Community: *Independent / Assisted Living. Levels of care offered. Cost goes up $400 for each additional level.*

Location: *Seaside, California*

Owner: *Jonathan Downey*

Location of Owner: *Seaside, California*

General Manager: *Bob Dunston-has been on staff for 4 years*

<u>Buy In</u>: *No*

<u>Rental/Lease</u>: *Month to month rental*

<u>Size/Accommodations</u>: *128 apartments ranging from 600 sq. ft. to 1200 sq. ft. 14 cottages ranging in size from 1000 sq. ft. to 1400 sq. ft.*

<u>Price Range</u>: *Ranging from 1900 to 4300 depending upon size and care needed*

<u>Pets allowed-Pet Deposit</u>: *Small pets allowed, $400 pet deposit-non refundable*

<u>Move in Deposit</u>: *$500 move in deposit-fully refundable*

<u>How often rent raised?</u> *Annually, between 4-7%*

<u>Current Occupancy</u>: *97% occupied*

<u>Proximity to Medical Facilities/Hospital</u>: *Sparrows Hospital 5 miles away. Physicians and Dentists within walking distance.*

<u>Nurse on Staff?</u> *No*

<u>Meals included in rent?</u> *2 meals per day. Resident can have additional meals for an added fee*

<u>Full Time Activity Director?</u> *Yes with assistant.*

Types of Activities: *Trips, classes, dancing, book clubs and outreach to community*

Smoking Allowed? *Non-smoking building, but there is a Gazebo on the property for smokers.*

General Comments: *Located in a residential neighborhood, 1 block from a high-end mall. Dog Park closely. Community has won many awards for the best retirement community in a small city.*

Many locals have moved there even though there are 5 other choices within 25 miles.

Report cards can be customized according to individual needs. Order form in back of book.

Chapter Twelve
Helpful Contacts

The courage to imagine the otherwise is our greatest resource, adding color and suspense to all our life.

- Daniel Boorstin

The following is a list of important contacts:

American Association of Homes and Services for the Aging

901 E Street N.W., Suite 500
Washington, DC 20004-2242
Phone: (202)783-2242
Fax: (202)783-2255
Web: www.aahsa.org
Phone: (203)237-4556
Fax: (203)237-4908

Access America for Seniors

This site offers links to various OTHER RESOURC-
ES for seniors: http://www.seniors.gov/

Ombudsman in Your County

The Ombudsman is a volunteer employee of the
County. This person advocates and problem solves for
senior residents; works with other city and county depart-
ments to resolve problems related to senior living. Individuals living in senior living communities have access to this
representative. Telephone numbers for this department
are posted in each community. The Ombudsman will seek
to resolve complaints that an individual may have about
their community.

Social Security Administration

This site provides a complete directory to all of the
information pamphlets and fact sheets that SSA publishes
on its benefit programs, including RETIREMENT, DIS-
ABILITY, MEDICARE, SUPPLEMENTAL SECURI-
TY INCOME, SURVIVORS BENEFITS, and information about your Social Security Number.

It also provides answers to over 400 frequently questions concerning social security: http://www.ssa.gov

National Institute on Aging

Offers much information on ISSUES CONCERN-ING THE ELDERLY, including publications on various health issues: http://www.nih.gov/index.html

National Association of Geriatric Care Managers

GCM is a non-profit, professional organization of practitioners whose goal is the advancement of dignified care for the elderly and their families. This website assists in FINDING APPROPRIATE CARE MANAGERS for the elderly: http://www.caremanager.org/

How to Order a Report Card

1) *Fill out order form online at*
   www.theparentcare.net

2) *Mail the form and check for $25.00 payable*
   to E. Morton to:

   E. Morton
   333 Mtn. View Drive, #138
   Talent, Oregon 97540

3) *Email the form to Emily Morton at*
   emilymorton53@yahoo.com

Report Card Order Form

Name:

Address:

_____

Type of Community Desired:

Location:

Time frame:

Level of Care Needed (Independent Living, Assisted Living, Nursing Home, or Memory Care/Alzheimer's Unit):

Price Range desired:

Smoking Community:

Meals Included:

Owner:

General Manager:

Other information you would like:

Red Flags

When your Asking, Looking and Doing are complete you need to look at this list of possible "red flags."

If any of the following jump out at you think twice before making a final decision!

Appearance of Building
1. Dirty carpet
2. Weeds in landscaping
3. Dirty windows
4. Strong Odors
5. General Clutter
6. Building in Need of Repair
7. Food on floor in dining room area or in hallways?

Feeling You Get When You Enter the Building
1. Do the residents look happy?
2. Does the staff seem happy and content?
3. Is there a sense of calm?
4. Is there activity in the common areas?
5. Is there someone at the front desk to greet you?

Ownership & Management
1. Local Management-this is best. There is more accountability for staff. The owner is usually well-known in the area and stops by often to check on the community and well-being of the residents. I have heard local owners call residents and staff by name, ask about family members and take a genuine interest in what is going on.

2. Large corporation. In a large corporation the individual communities may be part of a portfolio including other business enterprises. This may mean that the senior living part of the business is pressured to be the money maker. This is where food budgets often get cut and staffing is minimized. Since these owners are usually thousands of miles away from the community they are not around to check on the care and status of the resident care.

Quality of Food Service
1. Lots of starches and little protein?
2. Are cheap cuts of meat served?
3. Are pre-packaged and factory prepared meals served?
4. Are the uniforms on wait staff soiled?
5. Look at table tops-are they smudged Are the tablecloths clean?

Residents & Staff
1. Is there high resident turnover
2. Are the residents generally healthy
(If not could indicate that they are not happy and being cared for properly)
3. Are residents hanging around the lobby with nothing to do?
4. Do you see any residents-is there activity?
5. How long has the General Manager been on staff?
6. Is there high staff turnover? If so, why?
7. Are staff members bonded and fingerprinted?